CW01509425

THE WEATHER'S GETTING VERSE

The Stomping & Storming Poems
of Andrew Peters
illustrated by Alan Larkins

To Jane,
with love
(OPS! THAT GRAMMAR!)

Andy (x)

SHERBOURNE PUBLICATIONS

ACKNOWLEDGEMENTS

THE ANT DOCTOR first appeared in *The Grasshopper Laughs, A Faber Book of First Verse* 1995. HEY DIDDLE DIDDLE first appeared in the *Radio 4/Poetry Society Young Poetry Pack* 1995. HEY DIDDLE DIDDLE, TIDY THE SKY, THE BULLY, SCHOOL RHYMES & SCHOOL TIMES, ED THE DREAMER, A TALE OF TWO CUPPAS were all recorded at the *BBC Poetry Festival for Children* and then broadcast in a *Radio Four Talking Poetry Feature* 1995.

ISBN: 1 872547 22 2

Poems: Copyright Andrew Peters © 1996

Illustrations: Copyright Alan Larkins © 1996

Published by
Sherbourne Publications, Sweeney Mountain,
Oswestry SY10 9EX, UK Telephone 01691-657853
Creative typesetting by
Celtic Publishing Services, Llangollen, Denbighshire LL20 7BS
Printing and binding by
Bookcraft, Midsomer Norton, Bath, Avon BA3 4BS

INTRODUCTION

After *Word Whys*, people all over the country have been asking when the new collection would come out. It took a while, but here it is! Many of these poems resulted from workshops in schools and festivals. They have been tried and trialled with audiences and readers as well as being used for GCSE coursework. I have tried not to define an age range for this book and pray that everyone from tiny to tottering can gain some delight or insight from these pages.

I hope you find the poems both entertaining and moving. The section at the back both introduces some background to the poems and gives follow-up ideas for creative writing.

Happy reading and good poeting!

Andrew Peters, May 1996

DEDICATION

To my delightful daughter, Rosalind.

Thanks again to Polly for her editorial machete and Dorothy for her faith in my work. I would like to thank Alan for his hard work on the pictures and Tony for his creative typesetting.

◊

This book could not have been written without the *Valuing The Arts* writer's award given by West Midlands Arts in conjunction with Shropshire County Council.

CONTENTS

The Weather's Getting Verse   7
The Bully   9
After the Tragedies   10
The Numbers Game   11
When I come to the Dark Country   12
What a Little *Villainelle*   14
Spring   16
A Spring Conceit   16
Autumn Rhythms   17
Said the Leaf   18
Leaves   19
Winter   20
Winter Image   21
A Tidy Poem   22
Cerebral Palsy   23
Hey Diddle Diddle   24
What to Do if You're Bored   25
The Customer   27
A Tale of Two Cuppas   28
Ed the Dreamer   29
A Recipe   30
The Vegetable Wedding   31
School Rhymes and School Times   32
Killing Time   34
To Say Aloud and Annoy Your Friends, Parents, Teachers   36
The Ant Doctor   38
Overheard on the Television   39
The Witness   40
Forestry Commission Meeting Minutes   42
The Weapon Man   44
Where Were the Experts When it Came to Kissing?   46
The Troubles   48
Notes on the Poems   50

THE WEATHER'S GETTING VERSE

(a cowboy poem - to be read aloud
in a Texan accent!)

We were feelin' under the weather
It was Johnny McCloud and his *rain* of terror.
All of a *sodden*
A man came ridin'
Over the rangin' sky
"The name is Blue," he drawled
And then he called out,
"It's time for McCloud to die!"
Lightnin' quick, he drew his gun,
With a *shower* of lead,
McCloud was dead,
And his ghost just drifted away.

It was high noon,
In the *Rainbow* Saloon,
For the Man with the Golden *Sun*.

7

THE BULLY

*t*he bully's thoughts
are like a grey-grim tower block,
instead of trees, graffiti grows
and every smile is under lock and key.

The bully's anger must be made a crime,
loitering with fists,
disturbing the face,
joy-hiding,
killing time.

The bully's eyes are tarmac-dark,
crushing all who dare to grass,
his driven mind an empty space
in a concrete-cold car park.

The bully's fingers make a fist of twisted spoons
stirring up a soup of hate
to cook us in,
his heart, the emptiest of balloons,
full of hot air,
unable to care;
has anyone got a pin?

AFTER THE TRAGEDIES

We are the ones
That make the arms
That blow the legs
Off girls and boys.

Yes, we are the ones
That make the films
That fill with thrills
And blood that spills
And kills and kills and kills.

Oh we are the ones
That make the guns
That kill the kids
Then blame the men
That bought the guns.

We are the ones
That kill our sons.

The Numbers Game

10 Bright, blessed, innocent, this child of ten

9 Purring through numbered lives now nine.

8 Then came hungry war and ate,

7 With cruel cat's play we were all

6 At sixes and sevens.

5 Fear took her alive.

4 What was it for?

3 To be free?

2 Say who

1 Won?

1 One

2 Needs to

3 Simply see

4 What our great fore-

5 Fathers saw – to live

6 One must cut out the sick,

7 Deal with the cancer, even

8 If it seems cruel, we will create

9 An ordered world, where all shall be fine,

10 Cheap the price, to lose a few children then.

WHEN I COME TO THE DARK COUNTRY

*a*s I walked out one evening soft,
High in the hills of brown,
I came across a wounded land,
A queen without a crown.

I went to take her in my arms,
To smooth her grassy brow,
Wrap her in a quilt of cloud,
Say *hush my little earth, sleep a little now.*

But she could only lie and stare,
With eyes of blackened lakes,
Her tears were rivers running red,
This hand! She cried, *is all it takes!*

She held my human hand in hers,
And I grew scared a while,
And I began to burn with shame,
And ran a crooked mile.

But men had come before me,
With hands of withered grey,

Hands to pour out perfect waste,
To waste the land away.

Rubbish, Rubbish everywhere
And not a soul could think,
Waving in the seas of green,
Drowning in this drink.

And night was trapped in dust-bin bags
That wrap her darkened skin,
They wrinkle, but they never fade,
Ah! What a mess we are in!

The queen was calling out to me,
I could not hear what she said,
The sky was coughing yellow clouds
For soon she would be dead

As I sat down, an endless night
Fell on the breathless hills,
And the land lay drowned by an ocean of hands,
As it spills and it kills and it kills.

WHAT A LITTLE VILLAINELLE

*m*y teacher said I was doing really well!
He made me sit in a special place
until the lesson was over, I was saved by the bell.

I had broken every record for bad spell-
ing, come last in every race.
My teacher said I was doing really well,

but I think he was lying, well…
he had this horrible frown on his face.
The lesson was over, I was saved by the bell.

I ran. He grabbed me by the neck! "I'm going to tell
your Mum and Dad you can't be one of the human race,"
my teacher said. "I was doing really well,

until I met you, the pupil from hell
who can't even spell, what a hopeless case!"
My life would soon be over, I was saved by the bell.

My ears were ringing as teacher tried to strangle
me, the head rushed in, hit him with the bell, pell-mell
My teacher said, "I was doing really well…"
then he fell over dead! I was saved by the bell!

Spring

What do you think of Spring?
I asked the tree,

A buddy brilliant idea!
He said to me!

A Spring Conceit

The head of the sun is tucked behind
A leather-grey book of the clouds,
She is caught up in this binding
Tale, and the room where we live is a shroud.

The trees are thick with writer's block
A billion of thoughts they cannot unfurl,
Their pencil buds are garrets of rock,
Scraping the sky in a winded whirl.

Rain pours down without any plot
'til the trees are filled with wings
Stacked up high in the library sky
Now the spring has a voice, how she sings!

AUTUMN RHYTHMS

Cold Rivers
Cats' Shivers
Leaf Skivers
Sky Divers
Air Shak-Attack-A-Make-Me-Quake
Sun Drinking Sky
Night Thinking Sigh
It's Over
Gone Clover
No Flowers
Now Showers
Blues
Flues
Autumn
Caught 'em

SAID THE LEAF

Said the leaf to the sky,
I would learn how to fly,
But I'm shaking like a leaf, do I dare?

Said the sky to the leaf,
It's a matter of belief,
Just jump into my blanket of air!

Then the sky sang,
Then the leaf sprang,
And the trees were empty and bare.

LEAVES

Leaves are like traffic lights.
On the trunk-road
Of slow-moving seasons,
They go
Green,
Yellow,
Red.
Summer stops!
The sun is switched off!
The trees become
A multi-coloured traffic jam!

Then,
A crazy wind drives straight through the forest tall,
Makes each and every leaf
To fall and crash
Into the pile-up of Autumn,

And we,
Hoot and holler,
Dive and dash,
Scream and dream
And jump in the mess of shining, twisted leaves,
This happy accident of once a year
Where no-one is hurt, and nobody grieves.

WINTER

*i*n the night,
Came a white horse to visit.
His hooves made no sound
As he covered the ground
And snow filled the land with its spirit.

(Czech)

Winter Image

Jack
Frost,
riding
his
icicle.

21

A Tidy Poem

right then! It's time to tidy up the sky!
That's enough of your cheek! Don't ask me why!
I have told you a thousand times today
To put every one of those clouds away!
Lord, you are sometimes such a pain!
And you're just not old enough to play with rain!

Hey! You heard me!
Leave those mountains
alone!
They're sharp, unlike you,
with a brain thick as stone!

And I don't care if you're
a God in Heaven,
It's no pudding for you
and bed at seven!

22

CEREBRAL PALSY

*m*ichael was an Angel, fallen to earth,
A shower of light that burned the manger,
Body twisted like straw by the birth.
Michael was an angel…

But all who saw him, gave the widest berth,
As if their lives were in mortal danger
From his bent wings, his bloated girth.

They brayed their spastic jokes, made his pain gel:
He prayed to forgive the hardness of the earth
Where walking cripples could not see, Unable
Michael was the angel.

HEY DIDDLE DIDDLE

Wash your ears! Mum said.
So I took them off,
And stuck them in the washing machine!

Clean your room! Dad said.
So I rolled it up,
And shook it out of the window!

Make the breakfast! My brother said
So I did –
With bits of balsa wood and modelling glue!

Watch those cars! My aunt said,
So I sat all day and all night.
It was better than watching TV!

Take your time! My gran said
So I packed up my seconds
And flew to the moon,
Where my best friend is a cow
And I eat with a silver spoon!

WHAT TO DO IF YOU'RE BORED

*t*ake a shower,
(From B&Q).
Make the bed,
(With modelling glue).
Dust the house,
(for fingerprints).
Put the kettle on
(The fence).
Draw the curtains,
(Use a felt tip).
Ring your friend,
(With a hula-hoop).
Whisk a milkshake,
(Off to the beach).
Toast the bread,
(Make a speech).
Lay the table,
(Not an egg).
Feed the cat,
(To the dog).
Batter the Fish,
(With a cricket bat).
Eat your dish,
(And the table mat).
Run a bath,
(Don't skip or hop).
Then get some sleep
(From the shop).

THE CUSTOMER

m
ind your own business!" said the wild-eyed man
Breathing into my flabbergasted face
"It's the holidays!" joked the wife, "a bit of fun!
You know what kids are like, all over the place!"
She cried, carried on serving me,
Tried to hide her bruises with make up and made up lies,
As if I had not seen what I had seen:
A boy in a necklock with fear in his eyes.

I spoke up, perhaps a foolish bravery,
Me, the stupid, do-gooding customer
Then left, leaving a madman even more angry.
Later, behind blind doors, drink would father
Another punch, one son grow to know and run
Father's business, hitting *his* wife, beating *his* son.

A TALE OF TWO CUPPAS

When I was a cup of tea,
I spent my time watching tea-v
especially
films on flying saucers,
tea-rex and other dinosaurs.

One day,
as I went out to play
a bitter cup of coffee
tried to mug me,

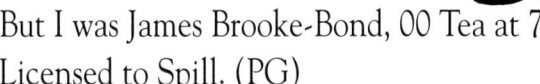

But I was James Brooke-Bond, 00 Tea at 7
Licensed to Spill. (PG)

I hit him on the head
with my tea-bag,
he fell down dead
and I ran away like a mug out of hell!

Then I met my perfect cup of tea!
Wow what a Beau-Tea! Such a Cu-Tea!
Her name was Sugar Lips, she made me laugh, Tea-hee!

And you might wonder if this poem can get any dafter,
but we made a stirring cup-ple and lived spoonily ever after!

ED THE DREAMER

"If you don't eat your greens right now!" Mum said,
"You'll end up thin as a slice of bread!"
Ed stuffed his face with dreams instead,
Thoughts to crunch and fears that fed
Nightmares into his head,
Got thin as a thread,
Mum cried, and led
him to bed
now Ed's
Dead
...............HUNGRY!

A Recipe

*t*ake a bunch of twinkling stars
And grab them by their shiny toes!
Pull them gently down to Earth,
Then stick them up your nose!

OUCH! and OW! They might shout out,
IT'S DARK IN HERE, IT'S HOT!
Wiggle them round with a pair of spoons,
Cover them well with snot!

Then pull them out with your fingers
Until they turn to chewing gum,
Sprinkle them with ear wax,
And squash them with your thumb!

Roll them flat with a rolling pin,
Then turn the oven on.
Ever so quickly shove them in,
And wait until they're done.

Ketchup, plate, sit and wait,
With soggy chips, what a treat!
They're ready, steady, hungry, go!
Yes! Bogey stars are great to eat!

And you might wonder why they're green,
But I can tell you where they've been!

THE VEGETABLE WEDDING

*t*he beetroot was getting married,
The celery squealed with delight.
The carrot stood up to dance a jig
And the horseradish whistled all night.

(Czech)

SCHOOL RHYMES AND SCHOOL TIMES

School! Oh! School is a feel-sick-won't-go place,
A stay-at-home-in-case-they-call-me-names-like-Pasty-Face place.

School! Oh! School is a can't-cry place,
A don't-show-your-tears-or-they-laugh-in-your-face place.

School! Oh! School is hate-in-wait-outside-the-class place,
A bully-words-of-stick-and-stone-to-break-my-bones place.

School! Oh! School is a teacher-tell-me-off place,
A *terrible-case!-Shoes-unlaced!-Hair's-all-over-the-place place*.

But,

School! Oh! School is a some-days-OK-place,
A best-friend-game-of-hide-and-seek-and-sardines place.

School! Oh! School is a tasty place,
A say-your-grace-yummy-plaice-and-chips-and-peas-please-on-Friday plac

School! Oh! School is an out-of-breath-run-and-play,
A climb-up-grown-up trees - *it's-ace!* place

School! Oh! School is an I've-won-first place! place
A best-in-the-race-with-the-fastest-pace-in-the-place place.

Oh! School! Yes! School is a sometimes hot, sometimes cold place,
A-Got-to-go, got-to-grow, get-to-know-it's-not-so-bad-after-all place.

33

KILLING TIME

Yesterday, I was bored, just killing time,
Today I'm busy, haven't got the time
because I killed time yesterday.

Yesterday, I was bored, just killing time,
I said *Let's hit the road, Let's hit town!*
So we fought through the rush hour,
battled through the jam
But then a driver carved me up, with a knife.
I'm falling to bits, what a life!

Yesterday, I was bored, just killing time,
I was hungry and I said: *I could murder a steak!*
And we did.

Yesterday, I was bored, killing time just like mad,
But then I found her something nice
And they'd slashed the price,
Beat their competitors and cut it in half, with a knife
What a bargain of a life!
Dressed to kill! Knock em dead!

Yesterday, I was bored just killing time,
I was mad when she said
It's over between us, let's knock it on the head
With a hammer, damn her.
The pain in her eyes
When she cut me down to size.

Yesterday, I was bored just killing time,
I was sad, so I went to a movie
'Cos I had to escape
From my life, with a knife.
It was a Hammer House of Horror
Where tomorrow never came, no it didn't;
All that violence on the screen did me in
And I had to walk out of yesterday.

Yesterday I got bored of killing time
It was bad. In the end I hit the sack,
Dead tired of
Killing time
Killing time
Killing time.

TO SAY ALOUD AND ANNOY YOUR FRIENDS, PARENTS, TEACHERS

a doggy stole a sausage,
From the big, bad butcher,
The butcher came and found her
And hit her with a hammer!
All the doggies cried,
They dug a little hole,
And on the doggy's gravestone,
They wrote this little tale:

A doggy stole a sausage,
From the big, bad butcher,
The butcher came and found her
And hit her with a hammer!
All the doggies cried,
They dug a little hole,
And on the doggy's gravestone,
They wrote this little tale:

A doggy stole a sausage,
From the big, bad butcher,
The butcher came and found her
And hit her with a hammer!
All the doggies cried,
They dug a little hole,
And on the doggy's gravestone,
They wrote this little tale:

etc!

(Czech)

THE ANT DOCTOR

*t*he Ant had broken her leg,
She bound herself up with a thread,
When the clock began to sing Midnight,
An Ant-Doctor ran to her bed.

The Doctor tapped on her heart,
And after, gave her this recipe:
Three times a day, a powder of sugar,
And soon you'll be better than best-can-be!

Miss Ant took the sugar-sweet powder,
Just as she had been told,
Each day she sat by the fire,
Each night she grew very cold.

She stayed in bed for four long days
On the fifth she started to cry:
Oh! Go away you bullying pain,
I do not want to die!

So then she blew on her broken leg,
And painted her toenails red!
Next morning, a happy and healthy Miss Ant,
Jumped right out of her bed!

(Czech)

OVERHEARD ON
THE TELEVISION

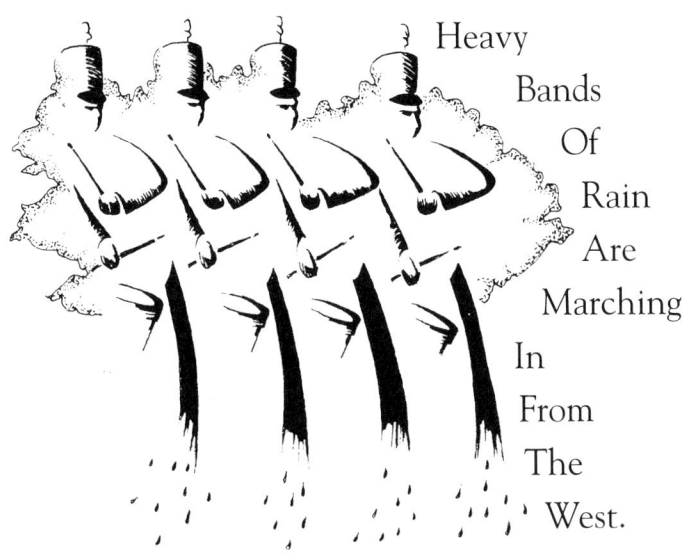

Heavy
Bands
Of
Rain
Are
Marching
In
From
The
West.

THE WITNESS

a man was driving home on the road
When, like a snake, the traffic slowed.
People were standing,
People were staring
For a car that had shed its skinny load,

Slipped like a scale, hit a girl in the back,
And the rush hour rush had fallen slack.
How he waited
With his breath bated
As a doctor prayed to give her breath back.

She lay like a rag doll coiled on the ground,
As inadequate onlookers stood around.
Then she was crying
Then he was sighing
With relief at a body that made a sound.

Give her a blanket, woven and warm,
To wrap up the thunder and muffle the storm,
The man was now sharing
As people stood staring,
Thankful that they had come to no harm.

People, minding their personal business
Shut their doors to the man and this mess,
Where death was dreaming
A girl lay screaming
In pain at the blood on her red, red dress.

At last came a woman with a blanket, cold
Out of the greenhouse, damp and old,
With a smile of false caring
As people were staring
At a girl worth less than growing mould.

Our souls are shops with doors shut tight,
Close up our hearts, turn out the light.
The girl was living,
But where was the giving
As day was sold to the grieving
night?

FORESTRY COMMISSION MEETING MINUTES

*i*t was decided on this day,
By the Venerable Alder Councillers
That a new forest was to be built.

Sadly, this meant that
Much of the town
Would be chopped down.

The people-mentalists were in uproar,
"Not In My Back Yard!" they screamed,
And the trees just dreamed.

To make matters worse,
The hours, years and minutes
Of the River Planning Sub-Commission
Were found to have given permission
To run a river right through
The new Housing Estate.

"Soon, there'll be streams all over the place,
Changing forever the face
Of our clean and concrete land!" they screamed,
And the trees just dreamed.

The FPCC members,
(An August Branch of World Interest Incorporated)
Listened to their words
Flying like leaves in the winds of opinion…

And saved the worst until last.
People would also have to be cleared,
Or it was feared
That good trees could be redundant.
But in appreciation of the people-mentalists' point of view,
It was agreed that all bodies would be recycled –
Leg cabins; fine finger bowls, unsoled foot-stools; complete head cases.
And it is our intention to give a helping hand to the armchair industry.

And so the trees that day, justly dreamed
And so the trees that day-dreamed, just dreamed.

THE WEAPON MAN

*O*n the flying plane,
I met a weapon man
How he was designing,
And now he was refining
A rocket, sock-it-to-'em
For his Fellow Man.

Weapon Man, Weapon Man, with arms in his hand
Weapon Man, Weapon Man, weeping on the Land.

On the lying plane,
I saw the Weapon Man
Soon they would be testing,
And bodies would be resting
In peace, as part
of a profitable plan.

Weapon Man, Weapon Man, blowing off the hand
Weapon Man, Weapon Man, crippling the Land,

On the sighing plane,
There sat a Weapon Man.
He was so excited,
His boss would be delighted
Wow, what a toy!
Biff! Boom! Bang!

Weapon Man, Weapon Man, shuffling his hand
Weapon Man, Weapon Man, beating the Land.

On the dying plane,
I heard the Weapon Man,
How his breath was rasping,
Now his heart was gasping
For life. A stroke of bad luck,
As his soul just ran.

Weapon Man, Weapon Man, dealt a dead hand
Weapon Man, Weapon Man, buried by the Land.

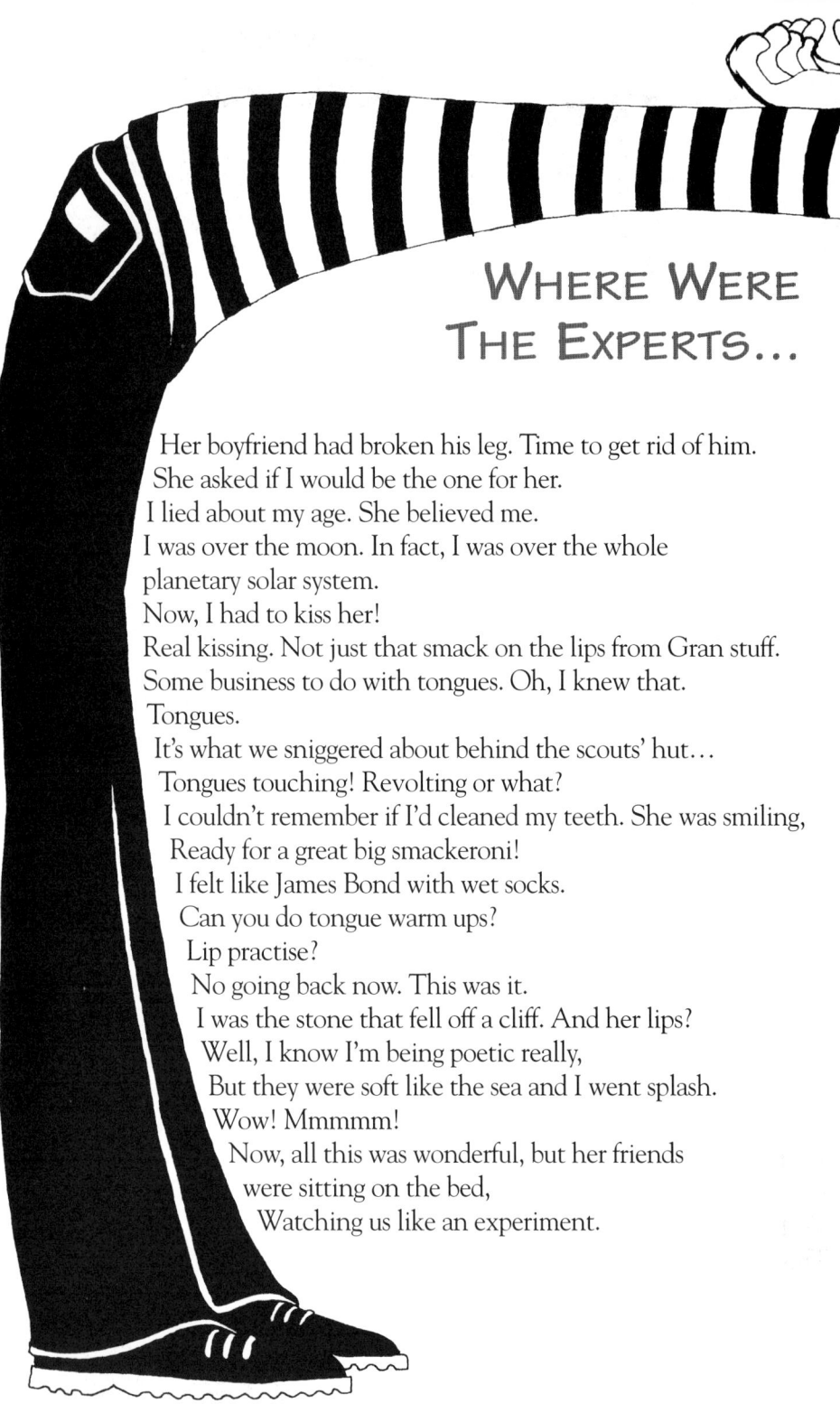

WHERE WERE
THE EXPERTS...

Her boyfriend had broken his leg. Time to get rid of him.
She asked if I would be the one for her.
I lied about my age. She believed me.
I was over the moon. In fact, I was over the whole
planetary solar system.
Now, I had to kiss her!
Real kissing. Not just that smack on the lips from Gran stuff.
Some business to do with tongues. Oh, I knew that.
Tongues.
It's what we sniggered about behind the scouts' hut…
Tongues touching! Revolting or what?
I couldn't remember if I'd cleaned my teeth. She was smiling,
Ready for a great big smackeroni!
I felt like James Bond with wet socks.
Can you do tongue warm ups?
Lip practise?
No going back now. This was it.
I was the stone that fell off a cliff. And her lips?
Well, I know I'm being poetic really,
But they were soft like the sea and I went splash.
Wow! Mmmmm!
Now, all this was wonderful, but her friends
were sitting on the bed,
Watching us like an experiment.

...When It Came To Kissing?

Completely offputting. There were several words I'd like
to have said, but this is a polite poem
and anyway, they were her friends.
Back to the kissing.
Technically speaking, our mouths were swapping spit,
And our tongues rolled around like wrestlers.
I found it hard to breathe.
It was great.
Five minutes went by.
Then another five. Then another.
You get the picture.
Limpets were wimps compared to us.
Half an hour now.
Her eyes were closed. She seemed to be enjoying it.
I began to panic. My tongue was drowning.
What if it died?
I mean, all this kissing wasn't too bad,
But I was exhausted.
Two hours later,
(I promise this isn't a brag, well not totally)
We finally ripped our lips apart and said goodbye.
I wandered round the town
With my tongue lolling out like a dog.
This must be love!

THE TROUBLES

What bombs, what fear
in a spring coiled tight,
snowdrops armed
with a lantern white?

The smash of steel
And tear of skin
a rip in the clouds
Where rain wears thin

The storm must end.

Listen to the hills,
Find another way
Where green and brown
both have their say.

Crop and fallow
Lie in their bed,
Ring of the hedge
Shall see them wed

The storm must end.

But cut the hedge
And steal the wind,
Then cage the trees
To cleanse the land.

This the human
Hand of hate
Filled with frost
For a spring too late

The storm must end.

Bursting the buds
Green on the brown
Arms of the tree
With a green-leaf crown

Bow to the sun,
Her bomb of light
Explodes on all.
Look now! Stop the fight!

Notes on the poems
...with follow-up ideas for creative writing

This section provides some background to each poem: why it was written, how I found the ideas and how it is structured. There are also suggestions for trying out your own writing. This includes where to find the inspiration and the idea for a poem, as well as how to go about it in an interesting and original way. Information is also provided on a selection of the traditional poetic forms, from the Sonnet, to Syllabic poems and Villanelles.

The notes for each poem can be read separately, but as a sequence, they also follow on from each other to develop good poetic building blocks.

◊

THE WEATHER'S GETTING VERSE is a poem resulting from a workshops about spring. I began my book with this poem because it is full of terrible jokes – especially the title – which is a pun which always gets groans from audiences.

A pun is a word that can mean one thing and yet sound like something else. It is a very short joke. So, in this poem, which is all about weather, we have: a *rain* instead of a *reign* of terror, and all of a *sodden* instead of all of a *sudden*. Different words with the similar or same sound are used in order to suggest different, funny meanings.

With these jokes, a poem doesn't have to be deadly boring. Everyone knows that the English are obsessed with the weather. However, a poem about the weather would be as dull and dismal as the clouds it describes. The trick is to make your subject interesting. So, I wrote about a storm as if it was a western gunfight (with a bit of James Bond at the end!). I personified the clouds (i.e. wrote about them as if they were a person) by turning them into a character called *Johnny McCloud*. I then tried to weave in as many stormy puns as possible. *Hailishly* difficult! A *rain* in the neck!

Try your own poem about the weather – but write it as a quiz show, a lottery programme, a cricket match – *the sun has been bowled out and the clouds (crowds) are really cheering. But rain stopped play!* etc.

◊

Poems can be found anywhere and **OVERHEARD ON THE TELEVISION** is exactly what it says. Individual words can have several different meanings according to the context in which they are used and it can be fun to really listen to what people say. If scattered showers were moving in – you might not want them as your new neighbours and if your friend said she was dying for a cup of tea, you might call an ambulance! See if you can find your own instant poem from a newspaper, a TV show, or just what somebody said to you. ''Found'' poems like this generally need a picture to bring out the humorous double meaning. Do some research and give it a go.

◯

THE BULLY uses these ideas of wordplay for a more serious subject. During my childhood and adolescence, I was often bullied, for being tall, skinny and for showing my feelings. It was one of the reasons I began writing. Words were the perfect revenge and you could never beat them up. This poem describes the Bully and there is a twist at the end which I will come to.

One of the first things about writing a poem is to use description. If I wrote: *I hate bullies,*
They are nasty
And I want to get them back,
…it may be what I feel, but it is a very dull poem. So, we need to find interesting ways to build our poem. I have already mentioned *puns* and *wordplay*. This poem goes a bit further.

The word *like* is a good place to begin. If I write, *the bully is hard*, I am not saying anything new. But if I say, *the bully thinks he is hard like steel*, it becomes more interesting because I am comparing one thing (the bully) with another (steel). This type of comparison is called *simile*. The use of simile can bring your ideas to life e.g. the sea. What is the sea like? You could say that *the sea is full of water*, but it is more creative to say – *The sea is like a plate, filled with a feast of water*.

THE BULLY came out of another workshop. We decided to build a bully with words to describe him/her. What did his anger look like; his eyes, lips, face, thoughts, dreams? *Lips like roads going on and on, driven by hate*. See if you can come up with your own descriptions. You don't just have to use *like*. *As* and *is* are two other poetic tools e.g. hard *as* rocks, or his heart *is* a stone. Using *'is'* to compare one thing to another is known as *metaphor*. A metaphor is a dressed up lie or a very different kind of description. The bully's mind *is* an empty space suggests that there is nothing between his ears. (see the notes on A SPRING CONCEIT about asking questions – why are the bully's eyes tarmac dark? etc.)

Again, I also used word play (*Joy-hiding, dare to grass, disturbing the face*) and built up the poem to end strongly. If the bully's heart was a balloon, how could we get rid of it? The last line answers the question.

All these ideas make what we call an *image*. Put the images together and you have written your own poem. One thing to always think about is how to finish your poem with a strong, concluding point.

◊

AFTER THE TRAGEDIES. In recent months we have all experienced horror, disbelief and great sadness in response to news of the most terrible tragedies. Our TV screens and newspapers have been filled with reports of the most dreadful random shootings in different parts of the world. I have a young daughter and, like every other parent, I am fearful about the world in which she is growing up.

I wrote this on the day an article appeared about Dunblane in a newspaper, next to an article on the same page about how the UK was selling new weapons to a certain country, saying, 'wasn't this good for business?' But this and other umimaginable horrs made me question the wider context. How many thousands of children have had their lives cut short by land mines that so-called civilized countries manufacture? And how many have been shot or maimed by weapons produced in the UK?

Could you write about these tragedies, or an event that has affected you greatly? Violence now is never far away from us. Not just on television, and in our films, but down our street and in the playground. It is a topic we don't generally write poems about. Maybe we can break that unwritten rule. Remember, words are powerful.

◊

WHEN I COME TO THE DARK COUNTRY. Ballads are one the oldest forms of poetry. Many were written as lyrics to be sung or spoken aloud and they often told a story, almost always with a gloomy ending (it's our horrible weather again) about ghosts, highwaymen, sad love affairs or historical battles.

The form of the ballad is often quite simple. It is made up of *verses* of four lines. Each verse rhymes on the second and fourth line, i.e. in verse one *brown* and *crown*. Each line is also broken up into *feet*. Feet is a very strange word that poets use to describe rhythm. But it makes sense, if you try walking along and saying the poem at the same time. A single foot may be made out of one or more beats or syllables – so in the first verse we can count the feet where it sounds like the natural divisions lie.

> As I/Walked out/One even/ing Soft
> High in/The Hills/Of Brown
> I came/Across/A wound/ed Land
> A Queen/Without/A crown

As you can see, there are four feet, or units of rhythm, in lines 1 and 3 and three feet in the rhyming lines. When you read a ballad aloud, it seems to flow along quite easily. This is the trick when writing your own ballad. Another way of finding the right rhythm is the very scientific *dum-de-dum* method. This is where the 'dum' lands on the syllable or word you stress most when speaking aloud. Thus, if we translated the first verse, it would go like this:

> de-dum, de-dum, de-dum, de dum
> de-dum, de-dum, de-dum,
> de-dum, de-dum, de-dum, de-dum,
> de-dum, de-dum, de-dum,

This way of translating your words can be very helpful to check the rhythm of your own balladeer attempts.

I wrote **WHEN I COME TO THE DARK COUNTRY** after a long walk in the countryside where I live. Everywhere I went, I could not get away from man-made mess, from barbed wire, to sweet wrappers to the ever-present coughing song of the cars. I imagined the earth as a beautiful woman being poisoned and perhaps my imagination is close to the truth.

Now that you know the background and structure, you could try your own ballad. Take a local myth, ghost story, or even your own pollution tale and turn it into a ballad. You could even try setting your words to music and becoming famous!

◊

THE NUMBERS GAME was written in response to Bosnia, and is about how often children suffer in wars started by childish adults. As you can see, this poem (and ED THE DREAMER) are both Syllabic or shape poems. The word syllable has three syllables or beats in it SYL/LA/BLE. A syllable is like the atom of which all writing is made up. (Count the syllables in the previous sentence – 17 I think!).

This poem begins with ten syllables on the first line, then nine, eight, etc., down to one syllable and back up to ten. The shape of the poem can often reflect the meaning. The poem is all about numbers, numbers of children being killed, numbers of adults justifying their actions. The rhyme scheme is also very concise. Each line rhymes with the number on the left hand side. (Apart from two lines. Can you spot them and the reason why they don't rhyme?)

Try your own syllabic writing. Take any sentence and then rewrite it, starting with one syllable on the first line, two on the second etc.

> *I felt so angry that I beat up the sky and moon and stars*
> would become…

53

I
Felt so
Angry that
I beat up the
Sky and moon and stars

Where it becomes harder, is when you also try to introduce rhyme. Give it a try and experiment with different shapes.

The poet George Herbert created many of these shape poems, some to look like bird wings, some like a diamond. For instance, a diamond would begin like the example we just tried, where each line gets longer by one syllable until it reaches nine or ten syllables in the middle, then it goes back down to one. (so 1234567898765432I is the syllabic count). Give it a go. As you will find out, it is hard work to fit it all together and still make it sound good…

WHAT A LITTLE *VILLAINELLE* is an even more complicated structure. The title is a wordplay on *villain* and the poetic form of the *Villanelle*. In this form, the first and third lines from the first *stanza* are repeated at the end of all the other stanzas. The poem is made up of five three-line stanzas and a *quatrain* (a stanza with four lines) to finish. The first and third lines of the first stanza keep being repeated in different order throughout, until they are put together in a final *couplet* (two lines that rhyme – see the sonnet, THE CUSTOMER). There is some poetic licence here – the last line is not exactly a repeat of stanza one, line three, but, as you will learn, all rules are made to be broken.

The *rhyme scheme* is also very ordered. A rhyme scheme is the way a particular poem rhymes. If you put the letter A at the end of the first line, B at the second (because it is a different rhyme), and A again at the end of the third line (rhymes with the first), you find the rhyme scheme of the first stanza – ABA. All the first five stanzas follow this ABA pattern with the last quatrain rhyming ABAA.

The whole point of a villanelle, is to use repeated lines which can take on slightly different meanings according to the context,. i.e. *I was saved by the bell* means one thing in stanza two, where it's an expression of being saved at the last minute, and another in the last line of the poem, where the pupil is literally saved *by the bell*. The villanelle can be a tough nut to crack and you need to be a real poetry addict to write one. The trick is to choose your first stanza with lines that can mean different things and write the poem based on this choice.

By the way, it's not an anti-teacher poem (I am married to a drama teacher – and she would soon beat me up if I was rude), but more a memory of a power-mad type of teacher I grew up with. In my work visiting schools, I rarely meet people like this anymore.

◊

SPRING. This one is a terrible joke. End of note!

◊

A SPRING CONCEIT came out of a writing workshop with top juniors – all about spring. *Conceit* is an old word that describes a set of images that are all linked to the same idea i.e. in this poem – the images I use to describe spring are all linked to books and words.

I changed the sun into an old woman (poets can take liberties with personification) and imagined her reading a book made of clouds. All the way through the poem, I was asking one question and it is a very important one for moving ideas forward. Why? Why is the sun reading? How does it make sense? Why do the trees have writer's block? The answers must help our poem along – if the sun is stuck behind the clouds, maybe it's because she is carried away reading her story. That's why it's cold down here, as she has let the fire go out. The trees have writer's block, because their leaves are stuck, unable to write on the sky.

Every image needs a reason. If we are going to write our own poem about spring, we need to answer some questions, i.e. if the wind is strong as a lion, then why? (maybe because it roars); if the snowdrops are white like paper – then why (maybe they get crumpled by the wind…). The clouds are grey like pavements – why? (you tell me). Try your own spring verse. Choose a subject – cars, a thriller, school, football, etc., and write your spring poem using only images from your subject, i.e. if it was cars, the wind could be driving the clouds mad, the trees could be like traffic lights (see the poem LEAVES which turns autumn into a car crash), the sun a Talbot Sunbeam, etc. Put all the images together and you have a *conceit.*

◊

AUTUMN RHYTHMS and SAID THE LEAF are poems which should work particularly well when read aloud. Try saying them to a friend, in class, in the mirror. As my aim was to make my images short as possible, with lots of rhythm and a good rhyme to finish (can you think of other rhymes for the word *Autumn,* or *Poem* for that matter?) SAID THE LEAF also uses one of the oldest poetic tools (also in many other of my poems) called

55

personification. As mentioned before, this is a poetic term for saying that the leaf, the sky and the trees are all described as people.

◊

LEAVES (See also notes on A SPRING CONCEIT). This is a conceit again, with all the images about a car crash. Again, I kept asking the question *why*? Why are leaves like traffic lights and why is autumn like a car crash?

I then develop the image and the question even further, because in asking why Autumn is like a car crash, I also ask why it isn't (nobody gets hurt). *Contradiction,* words that don't make logical sense when put together, is also a valuable poetic tool. Most accidents are unhappy, but I can describe Autumn as *a happy accident* and create a more startling picture. Try writing an Autumn poem with your own contradictions, i.e. *the trees are wearing a happy frown, this cold wind warms our hearts,* etc. If it sounds strange, it might make your poem more imaginative.

◊

WINTER is a traditional Czech nursery rhyme which I had great difficulty translating, to get the sense of rhythm and the music of the words.

◊

WINTER IMAGE is not my poem, but created in a brain-storming session in Greyfriars Primary School in Kings Lynn, Norfolk. I am also a word-burglar. We were working on thinking up puns about winter and this was the best. But the wind eating *a barkon & egg sandwich* wasn't bad either. See if you can come up with an even better pun.

◊

A TIDY POEM grew out of the thought that God might have a very fussy mum. I am most often inspired by weird and unusual ideas… I certainly wasn't intending any sort of religious insult , but was interested in my strange concept of God being a messy child who never tidies his room. His room, of course, is the world. Children and adults of all ages have enjoyed this poem and I hope you can see why.

Maybe you could write your own tidying poem. Where could you put the rivers? Could you fold them up? How about the forests – give them a good short, back and sides? What about the sprawling cities – they might need to be stuck in a washing up bowl and given a good scrub and rinse…

HEY DIDDLE DIDDLE and **WHAT TO DO IF YOU'RE BORED** are all about playing with the meaning of words in different contexts. Words like *wash, ring, take, draw, run,* etc. I tried to think of phrases that we use in everyday speech, and then twisted them to get the joke. We often say things without thinking about what the literal meaning is. So, *take a shower* – I could literally steal one, run off with one, buy one, etc. See if you can come up with your own phrases and make a joke out of them. (Also see notes on OVERHEARD ON THE TELEVISION)

A poem from my last collection **Word-Whys** was called *Street Signs*. I took all the street signs and imagined them being literally true – so *Kill Your Speed* (I stabbed my car in the bonnet!) *Dead Slow Children* (loads of children crawling down the road on their hands and knees).

◊

THE CUSTOMER. This poem is based on an experience I had on holiday last summer, when I went into a shop to buy some cheese. I was extremely upset by what I saw – a boy coming into the shop and the father pulling him around the door with great violence. What made it worse, was the mother who served me pretending it was all a joke. For the first time in my life, I did not stand by and pretend nothing was going on, but said to the man – "are you going to hit him now? I thought beating children went out with the Victorians…" My stupid comment made him even more angry, and if my wife had not been there, I think he would have punched me too.

I wanted to go the social services, do something, anything, as this is the sort of thing that is often simply ignored. In the end, I wrote this poem instead and maybe the positive message is that it is not hidden but out in the open. No-one of any age, should have to suffer like this.

I chose the traditional form of a sonnet. Through the ages, sonnets have often been used to express the big feelings of love (e.g. Shakespeare who dedicated his sonnets to the mysterious W.H), or sadness and loss. The tightness of the structure is one way to both contain and enhance the strength of feeling.

There are many different types of sonnets. THE CUSTOMER is based on the Shakespearean model in its rhyme scheme. As you can see there are fourteen lines divided up into two stanzas. The first, of eight lines, is called the *octave,* and the second, of six lines, the *sestet.* The rhyme scheme runs ABAB, CDCD, EFEF and ends with a rhyming couplet GG. (See WHAT A LITTLE *VILLAIN*ELLE for explanation of *rhyme scheme*) Generally, the lines are ten syllables long - though I have granted myself a special poet's licence to break the rules (as did many others – some of G M Hopkins' sonnets go up

57

to 14/16 syllables per line). The true art of writing is to learn the craft and then adapt it to your own skill.

The structure is immensely important for the power of the poem. The place where the octave and sestet divide is often known as *the turn*. The reason for this is simple. The idea is to turn the poem round at this point and introduce a different perspective which sheds light onto what has gone before. If the sonnet was a condensed detective story, the turn would be the moment of breakthrough when the finger pointed at someone who seemed completely innocent so far. Thus, here the poem changes from me observing this terrible situation, to suddenly speaking up and becoming involved.

The sadness is obvious. Although I have *turned* the situation, the foolish bravery has made no difference. Often the final rhyming couplet sums up and concludes the sonnet. It needs to be final and punchy, to make the point with the last rhyme. I hope this poem succeeds.

Look for the word-play and puns in the poem, where again words can have different meanings depending on context. Once you decide to write your own sonnet, choose your subject first – perhaps an event that has affected you greatly – some loss in the family, love, anger, etc. It is a good idea to do a rough map first by putting the rhyme scheme you have chosen (you can look up other types of sonnet) vertically down the right hand side of a blank page, leaving room for your first draft lines, i.e. a guide for the first four lines would look like this:

....A
....B
....A
....B

With this visual reminder, you know that you have to find the right rhyme for the last word of each line. Think about what you want to say, how your *turn* will change the poem. Writing of this complexity takes some planning. Very few poets just feel inspired and dash off an epic in five minutes. This is where the hard work begins, but such crafting brings its own rewards. Good luck!

CEREBRAL PALSY is a similarly crafted piece of writing, like THE CUSTOMER. This poem is written as a *roundel*: this was a very popular french verse and comes in many varieties. CEREBRAL PALSY is in a form made popular by the poet Swinburne.

It consist of three tercets (three line stanzas) with the first half line repeated as a refrain or tail at the end of the first and last tercet. The rhyme scheme is strict – if we called the refrain *R*, then the rhyme scheme would go *abaR, bab, abaR.* (See WHAT A LITTLE *VILLAINE*LLE for explanation of rhyme scheme).

The Roundel is exactly what it says, with the first line being repeated at the end, the poem comes full circle. The idea is that the repeat refrain is often a pun, or changes its meaning according to context in subsequent lines. Thus the last repeated refrain in this poem makes the point that the name callers and the prejudiced are unable to fly, and people like Michael have much clearer and honourable spirits.

The poem is based on some work I did with adults who have cerebral palsy. The project affected me greatly and I hope this poem does not come across as condescending. One of the group had very severe physical difficulties – Michael was sharp as a pin – but it was almost impossible for him to get his words out. He told me about one of the myths of the Severn River, named after Sabrina, who drowned men with her smiles…

When I thought about Michael, I kept seeing him as an angel. This idea formed the refrain and I tried to work the poem around it. It was particularly difficult to find rhymes for *angel* – I resorted to some half rhymes and the sound rhyme *pain gel* in the last tercet. Such tight rhyme can either make your poem sound contrived, or contribute to the lyrical quality.

If you make an attempt at this form, choose your refrain carefully – possibly a phrase that can take on different meanings. The poem is short, so you need to keep your images concise and keep drafting to produce a polished poem.

◌

WHEN I WAS A CUP OF TEA has been a favourite with audiences all over the country. Why? Because it is really daft! See if you can do your own poem about being turned into something strange – like a car(he *drove* me mad! I was *exhausted!*) or a tree – (on her way to meet a *bark, handsome stranger!*) How many jokes can you fit into your poem? Puns and jokes are not just silly. They can be a wonderful way of stretching your wordability. Also, it goes to show that POETRY DOES NOT HAVE TO BE BORING.

◌

ED THE DREAMER is another syllabic poem (see notes on THE NUMBERS GAME for structure and ideas). I set myself the challenge of having every shortening line end with the same rhyme. The shape gives the game away. Dreamy Ed, and the poem about him, are both getting thinner. It could even be a sad ending. But it wasn't. Ah! If you are going to do your own syllabic poem – you need to choose your shape to fit the subject or an image you want to use, e.g. a poem about a baby brother/sister who had eyes like diamonds means you could use a diamond shape for your poem, etc.

◊

A RECIPE. There had to be at least one poem with snot in it. Bogeys are the perfect subject for an edible poem. You are allowed to write at least one disgusting poem in your life. This is your only chance. If a serious adult poet can do it – so can you and much better.

◊

SCHOOL RHYMES AND SCHOOL TIMES is a poem with two sides to it – partly based on my memories of going to school. I began the poem with all the bad feelings I remembered – of being teased, told off and generally feeling miserable. The word *BUT* in the middle of the poem changes it completely, giving the other side of the story. The traditional words for this type of double poem are *ODE* and *PALINODE* or you could almost think of it as *poison* and *antidote*.

I linked the two halves of the poem with the same rhyme – which took a long time to structure. Try your own poem about school, writing about both the good and the bad aspects. Choose a simple word that has loads of rhymes for it, e.g. *bet – school's as bad as a bet I've lost, it's always wet, each exam they set, I fail*, etc. But don't forget to turn the poem round and have a positive ending. One way to help with the rhyme is to go through the letters of the alphabet and stick them on the front of the sound of your word to see if you can make other words, i.e. with bet aet, bet, cet, det eet, fet, get, let, met, net, pet – some of the words are nonsense – but as you go through and gain confidence, try longer words – adept, inept, Annette! You could also find these rhymes if your school or home computer has a rhyme programme, or look out for a rhyming dictionary.

◊

THE VEGETABLE WEDDING is one of my favourite Czech nursery rhymes. As I have said, I enjoy impossible and crazy ideas. Can you find any traditional rhymes from your own culture and background? (Mums, Dads, Grans, etc., are great rhyme providers – do some investigation/translation. If everyone in your class went home and did some research, there could be an amazing traditional poetry sharing day…)

◊

KILLING TIME is another poem about everyday phrases we use without thinking. Our conversation is filled with violence, and all I did with this poem was to bring out this theme. The use of rhythm emphasises the power of this piece which began life as a performance poem but works well on the page. Try reading this poem aloud to hear the rhythms and then discuss the emotional impact of it.

Try a day of listening to other people's and your own conversation and see if you can pick out any violent phrasing – *she's tearing me apart, he had me in stitches, we shall beat the cutbacks, it's a war out there,* etc. See if you can weave them into a rhythm or group poem by taking the phrases and bringing out their latent meaning, i.e. above *he had me in stitches, the operation took hours. We beat the cutbacks, with a baseball bat.* Good practice when drafting poems is to read each draft aloud to yourself. Does it flow? Could you change an image, or a word to fit the rhythm? Practice makes better.

◊

TO SAY ALOUD is exactly that – a traditional Czech circle rhyme – you can keep saying it over and over. Experiment! You too could be a pain! Can you find any examples from your own cultural background – in stories or poems. Are shaggy dog stories still around? (see also THE VEGETABLE WEDDING)

◊

THE ANT DOCTOR. The Czech nation, like many countries, have a wonderful tradition of myth and rhyme where animals have human characteristics. e.g. the English Lewis Carrol's rabbit in Alice in Wonderland, Ratty from Wind in the Willows, etc.

◊

THE WITNESS. I wrote this poem in frustration and with sadness after coming upon the scene of a traffic accident. I think the words speak for themselves. As in many of my poems I was keen to find a structure to contain or carry my feelings and this is a form of my own making (but I am sure it's not original). What saddened me most about the event was not the shock of the blood, or the accident itself, but the way some of the onlookers just seemed switched off. I changed the gender of the man who found the blanket – poetic licence again – but he and his mouldy blanket do exist and I dedicate this poem to them both. The girl was later apparently not too badly injured, but *kindness was the victim of a hit and run.*

FORESTRY COMMISSION MEETING MINUTES . What if you reversed everything? Changed around the forest and the city. *A forest of skyscrapers. A city of trees.* This poem could be one result. By playing with ideas of reality, I am hopefully making an ironic point about destruction of our environment. Laughter in the form of *satire* can be a good weapon. Satire is a way of exposing stupidity through making fun of it.

Once I had fixed on this technique of reversal, then all my language had to follow this idea. The power of the poem then lies in the use of puns and word-play to fit this alternative reality together. Thus, houses can be *chopped down* as though they are trees and *people-mentalists* has a double joke in it... Also, if people had to be recycled – there could be lots of jokes to do with parts of the body. Once again, I am exploring how our conversation is often littered with phrases that by dictionary definition can mean two different things – armchairs made out of arms, etc., and the awful pun of *leg cabins*. (very groan-worthy)

Plan your own reversal poem – maybe *river and road (I went to find the source of the road, but all I could see was a tarmac spring, etc.), city and sea, day and night, house and nest.* The trick of a good final poem is how cleverly you work your changes. You must make the reader believe in the surreal world you have just created. It can also be a more interesting way of making a moral/environmental point.

WEAPON MAN. I was flying into Washington DC, and the man in front was chatting to his neighbour all about the wonderful new weapon he had been working on. The second man was keen to seem interested and the conversation went on in businesslike but friendly terms as they talked about a rocket that kills people. Ah, the joys of civilisation! I was too cowardly to make some sarcastic (but poetic) point as he left the plane. Instead, I took my revenge in this poem.

The structure (see notes on KILLING TIME) gives the poem life when read aloud. This poem, BALLAD OF THE EARTH and THE TROUBLES have already been set to music. This might be a possible creative response to these poems – coming up with a tune with whatever instrument you play – singing, rapping, speaking the words, sampling them – many possibilities here.

As you can see, each verse is followed by a chorus – which changes slightly each time. Each verse follows the same structure. Work out what it is and why I have slightly changed the first line each time. Does it add to the meaning? Why? Does the rhythm add to the power of the poem?

Perhaps initially, try speaking the words in front of a group – with different voices for each verse, a large group for the chorus or alternate lines of each verse in pairs. Have someone whispering/chanting/humming the first chorus in the background all the way through. Maybe add in some clapsticks or basic clapping rhythms. Take some risks. Improvise. Find what works.

The idea is to try and build atmosphere with the use of sound. Poetry readings can often be dull. But this stereotype deserves a sudden death. Delivery, performance and timing can give a wimp verse huge poetic biceps that will impress every audience and make them gasp for more.

More seriously though, the tradition of poetry was not in books. Beowulf and the Canterbury Tales were bawdy, moving, irreverent, spiritual – traditionally set to music and told in front of fires roaring like lions on cold nights – poetic tales to make you laugh and cry. Now we have the National Lottery Live and the box of a thousand dead dreams.

◊

WHERE WERE THE EXPERTS WHEN IT CAME TO KISSING? is a title that is almost long enough to be a poem by itself. Another story - this one of my first love and no, I am not going to tell you her name or how old I was, so don't be cheeky.

After so many formal poems, I needed a break. So this poem has virtually no rhyme. But (and this is an important but) it still reads well. For me, a poem has got to look and sound right before it is finished. Drafting can be tedious, but it is worth the effort.

Here, I wanted to tell a story – the tale of my first kiss.

I won't say much more – except about the imagery. When I work in schools, people often ask me to read their poems and some of these are love poems. I am always happy to give feedback, but I sometimes cringe when a crumpled poem is shoved in front of my face.

It is nearly always guaranteed that *hearts will be broken, lips will be red as roses, eyes will seem deep as pools and nearby, trees will sway softly in the wind.* When I read stuff like this, it makes me want to vomit. Excuse my rudeness! It is not the writers I am upset about, but their use of language. Phrases like those above are like a steak cooked to death – rubbery, old and I can't get my teeth round it. People can often think, *but this sort of language is poetic and I am writing a poem.* Rubbish! This sort of language is filled with clichés and if we are to work on our poetry, this if the first thing we must discard when we re-draft.

That was the negative. Now for the positive. Take your clichés and twist them. Trees swaying like… drunkards, heart broken like… a plate, and now I am fragile, sharded, discarded etc. Then, old language can be like the phoenix and rise from the fire. So, in this poem, I tried to come up with original images – *I felt like James Bond with Wet Socks, Tongues rolling around like wrestlers.*

If you are going to write a love poem, then take time to build your images and make them interesting. If she has dark hair – dark like what? – *dark like done days, like shadows that entice me, like old rooms but will she ever let me in?* Describe his/her hair, eyes, beauty, heart, feelings. Think about the shape of your face when you smile or cry. Smile *like a moon, cradling the stars, like a banana, and I always slip up on my words.* Each time you find an image, develop it – if something is like something else, then why? Answer the question (See notes on A SPRING CONCEIT) and you will end up with a distinctive poem.

The images you find (like my tongue description) can be unusual. In one workshop – we tried some strange similes and the group came up with *hair, messy like an oil spill, what a complete tanker!* As an exercise, take a subject – love, eyes, a relationship. Then, look around the room or outside and choose any four objects. Put the two together, i.e. *Love is a table* – why? *Because I feel flat sometimes and just want to leggit,* etc. With all these ideas in mind, you could be well on the way to the ultimate love poem to impress that special person.

◊

THE TROUBLE. This book ends with a poem about Northern Ireland. I am no politician and would never presume. But there is too much prejudice in the world, from bullying to fighting and war. I pray, idealistically, that there could be another way.

I was walking in the Shropshire hills near where I live, and had one of those odd poetic thoughts I get once in a while: the clouds don't fight with the sun, I thought and that was the germ of this poem. I tried to use this language of violence (see KILLING TIME) to describe nature. Nature is violent, angry, full of explosions – but this warring of the heavens only rarely kills to the extent that we humans do. Our wars can do more damage and last longer than any flood or volcano.

Again, this poem is written in a lyrical structure (see THE WITNESS) and has been set to music. You could try putting these or other words to a musical form, or even write your own peace lyric, the ending of which is up to you. May your writing take wings – and remember, words are powerful!

64

Biography

Andrew Peters is an Anglo-Czech author and poet well-known within education and the media. For ten years he has been performing and running workshops on poetry and storytelling. "Part of the success must lie with Andrew Peters' charisma and youthful energy." TES

His poems have appeared in many anthologies, including more recently – Custard Pie (Macmillan), A Faber book of First Verse and the Radio Four/Poetry Society Young Poetry Pack. His poems have been broadcast on Poetry Please, Talking Poetry, Kaleidoscope and Blue Peter.

Andrew's first collection – **WORD WHYS** (Sherbourne Publications) was published in 1992. It is currently being translated and will be published in Poland in 1997.

In 1993, his brother Mark, a successful poet and editor based in America, died of AIDS. A book of Mark and Andrew's poems **MAY THE ANGELS BE WITH US** and accompanying teacher's pack were launched by Shropshire Education Services on World AIDS Day 1994. The book went on to gain national acclaim, with features from Kaleidoscope, the Guardian and TES.

"Your poems make me wish that I had known your brother. But then his own work triumphantly survives him." Sir Ian McKellen

"A handsomely produced and warmly illustrated book, enthusiastically endorsed by actor Alec McCowen available for the peanuts price of £4.50 only by mail order from Shropshire County Council, which took not only the bold decision to publish, but is giving all profits to the Shropshire and Mid Wales Hospice." David Ward, The Guardian

1994 saw Publication of **SALT IS SWEETER THAN GOLD**, a traditional Czech folk tale illustrated by Zdenka Kabatova-Taborska with Barefoot Books in Great Britain and USA. It made the list of National Tell A Story Week, and was a Harpers & Queen Christmas book choice. "Andrew Peters' narrative is rich and evocative", Montessori Education. "…bold and colourful", The School Librarian. "…a touching tale, full of colour and Eastern European style", Kids Out.

In 1995 Andrew published **A SHROPSHIRE GARLAND**, a sonnet sequence of Shropshire Poems with illustrations by Jane Keay.

His **BAREFOOT BOOK OF STRANGE AND SPOOKY STORIES** is coming out in 1996/7 and other story books are published by Ginn and Harper Collins. He is also an accomplished musician, with his film library music published and broadcast worldwide through Sonoton.

Andrew lives in a small Shropshire Village with his wife and young daughter.

Notes On The Illustrator

Alan Larkins is a freelance artist/illustrator living in Oswestry, Shropshire, with his wife and daughter. Alan is at present studying Art at the North Shropshire College.